Come to

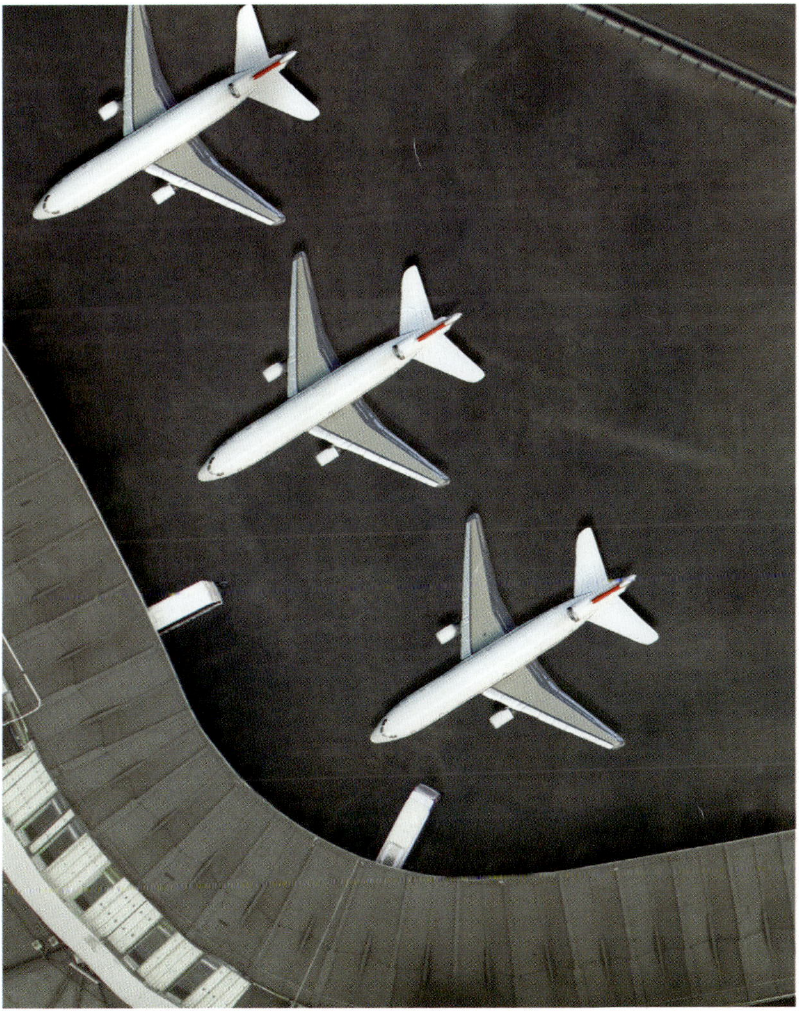

written by Pam Holden

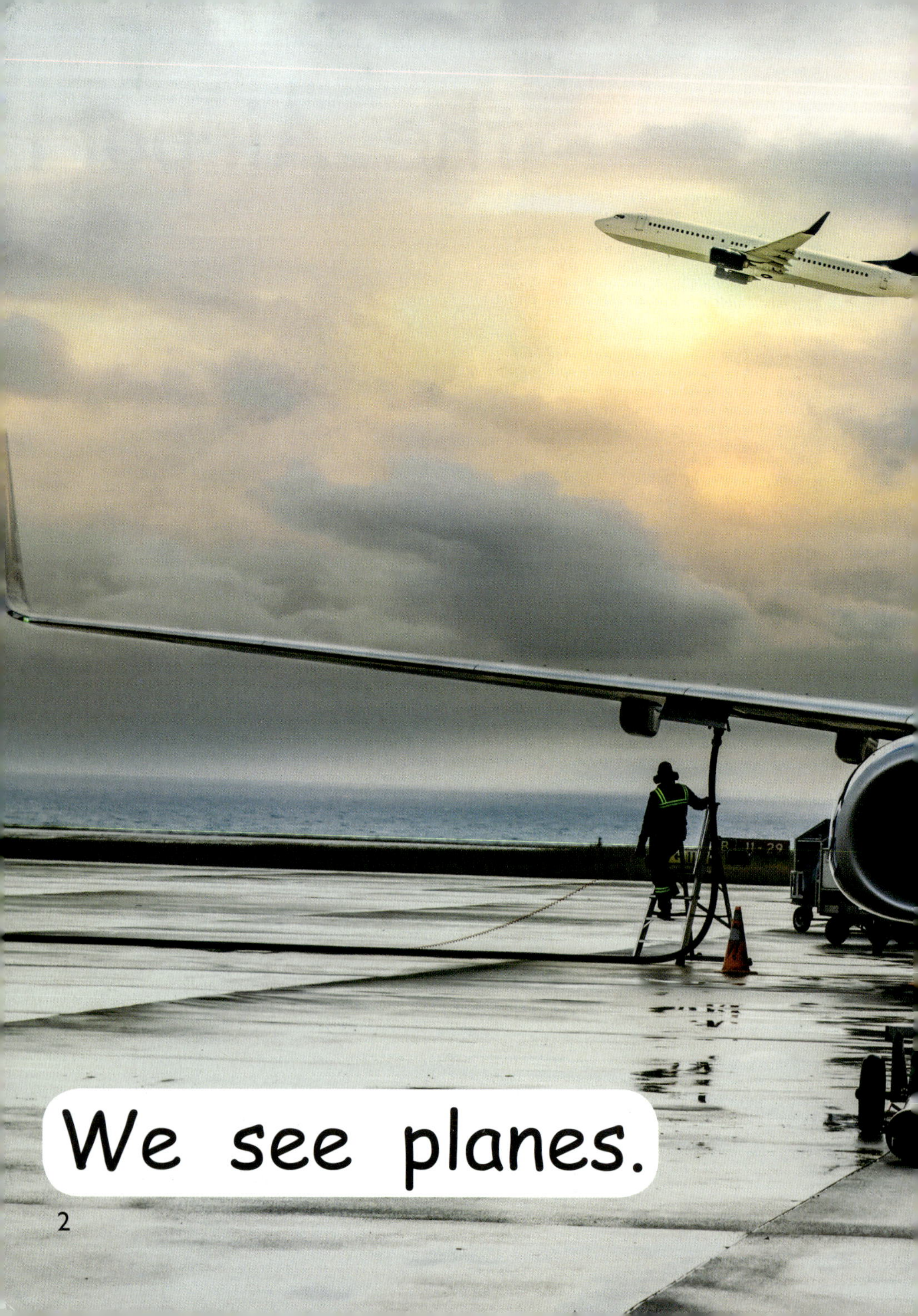

We see planes.

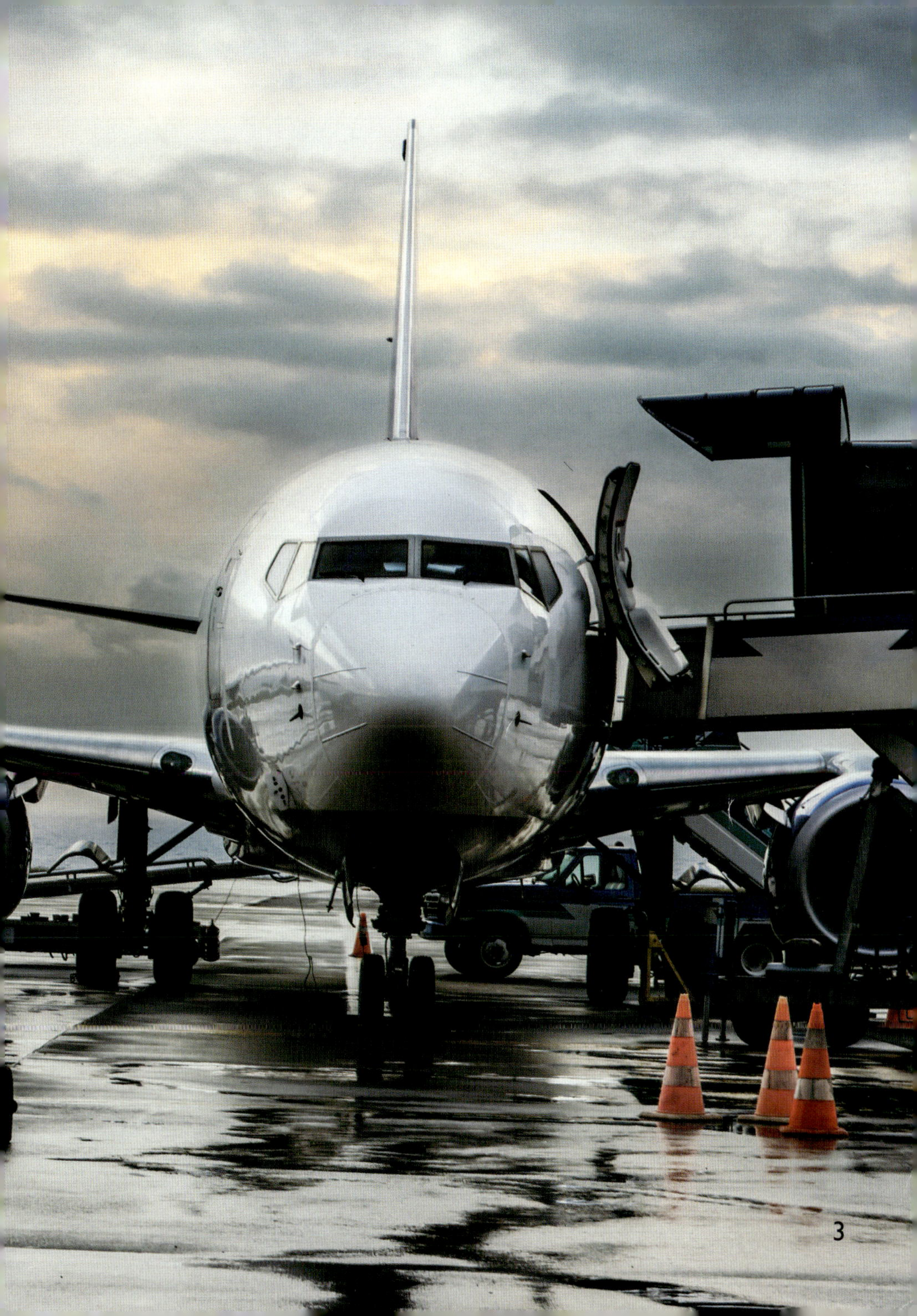

We see a runway.

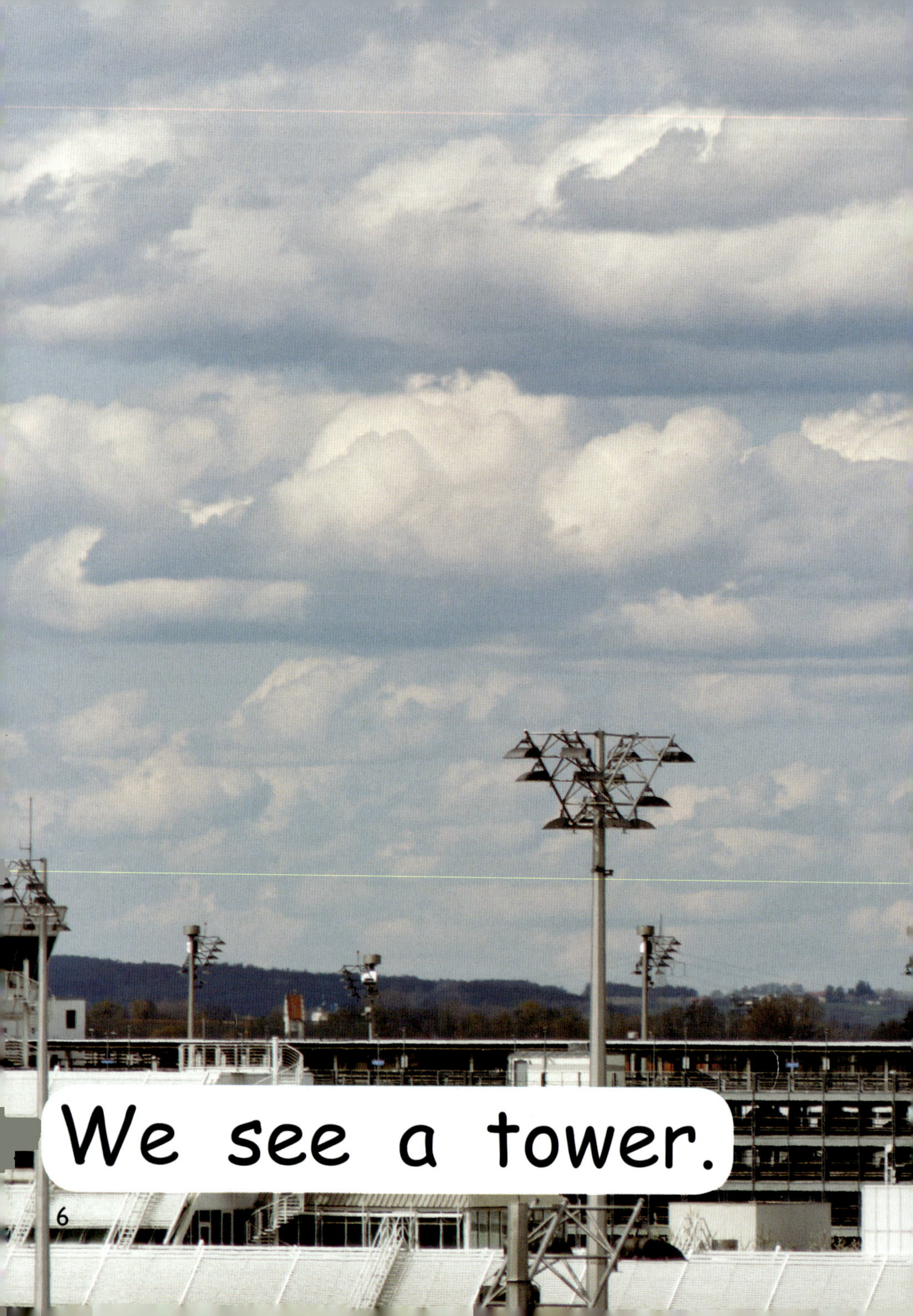

We see a tower.

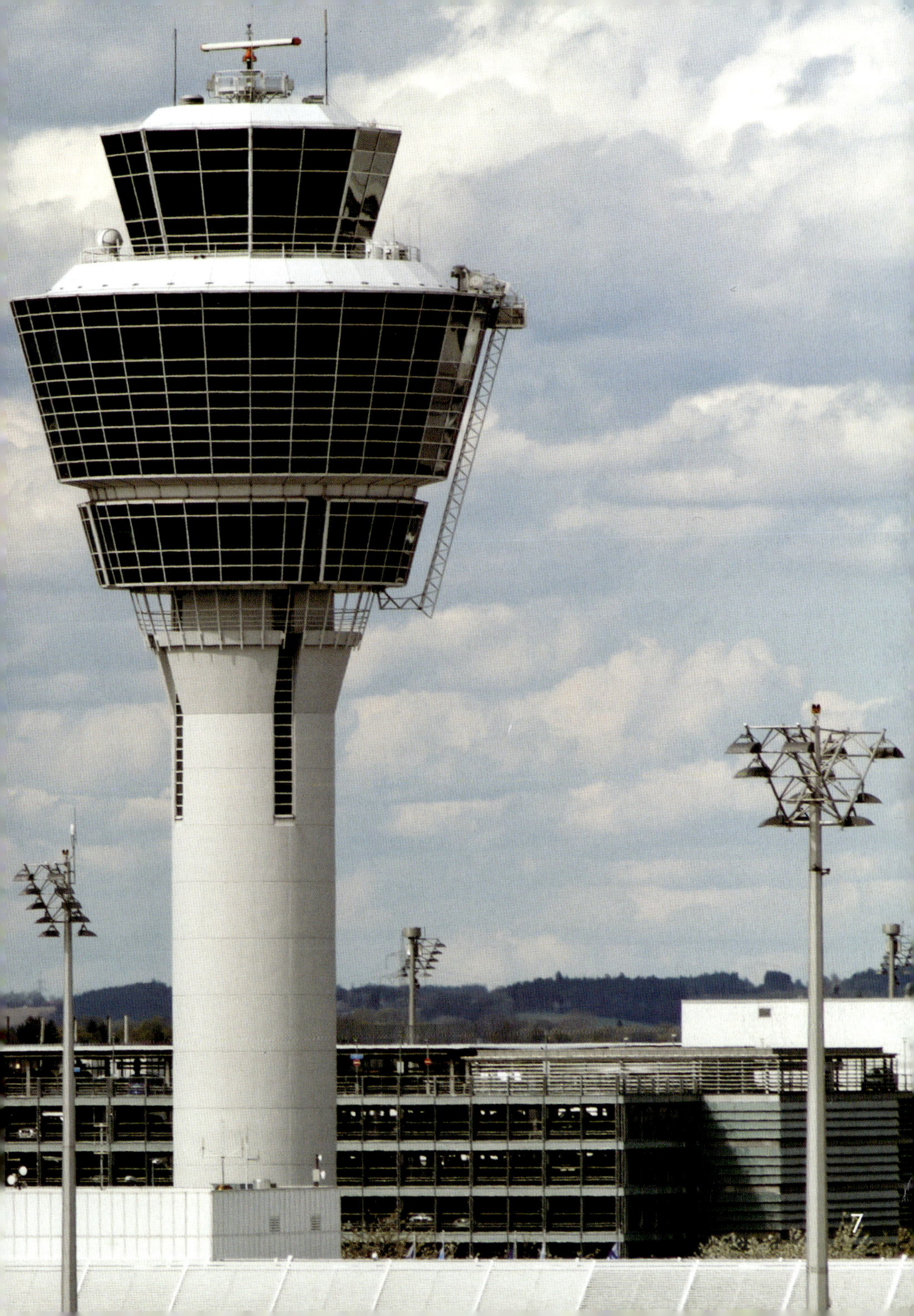

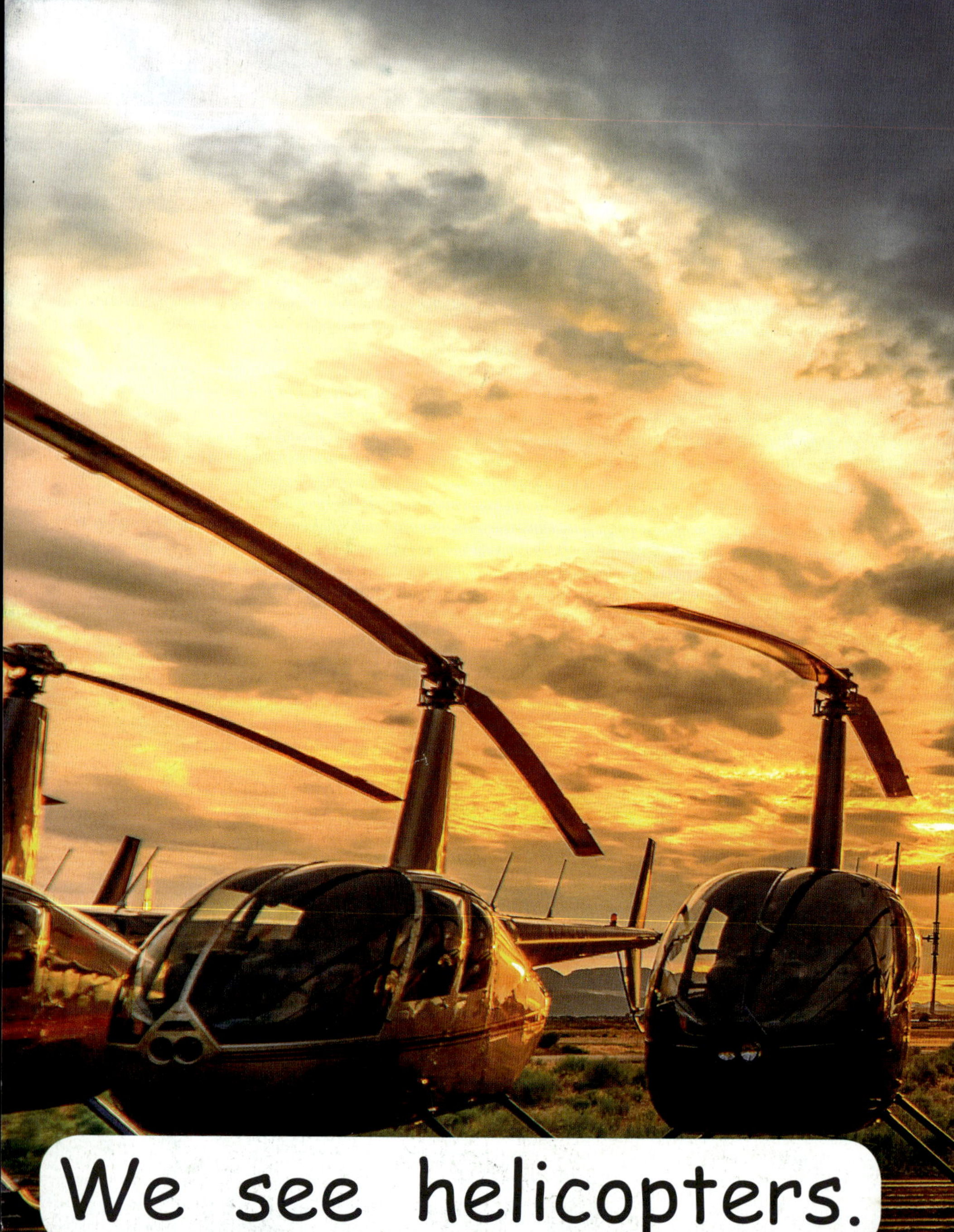

We see helicopters.

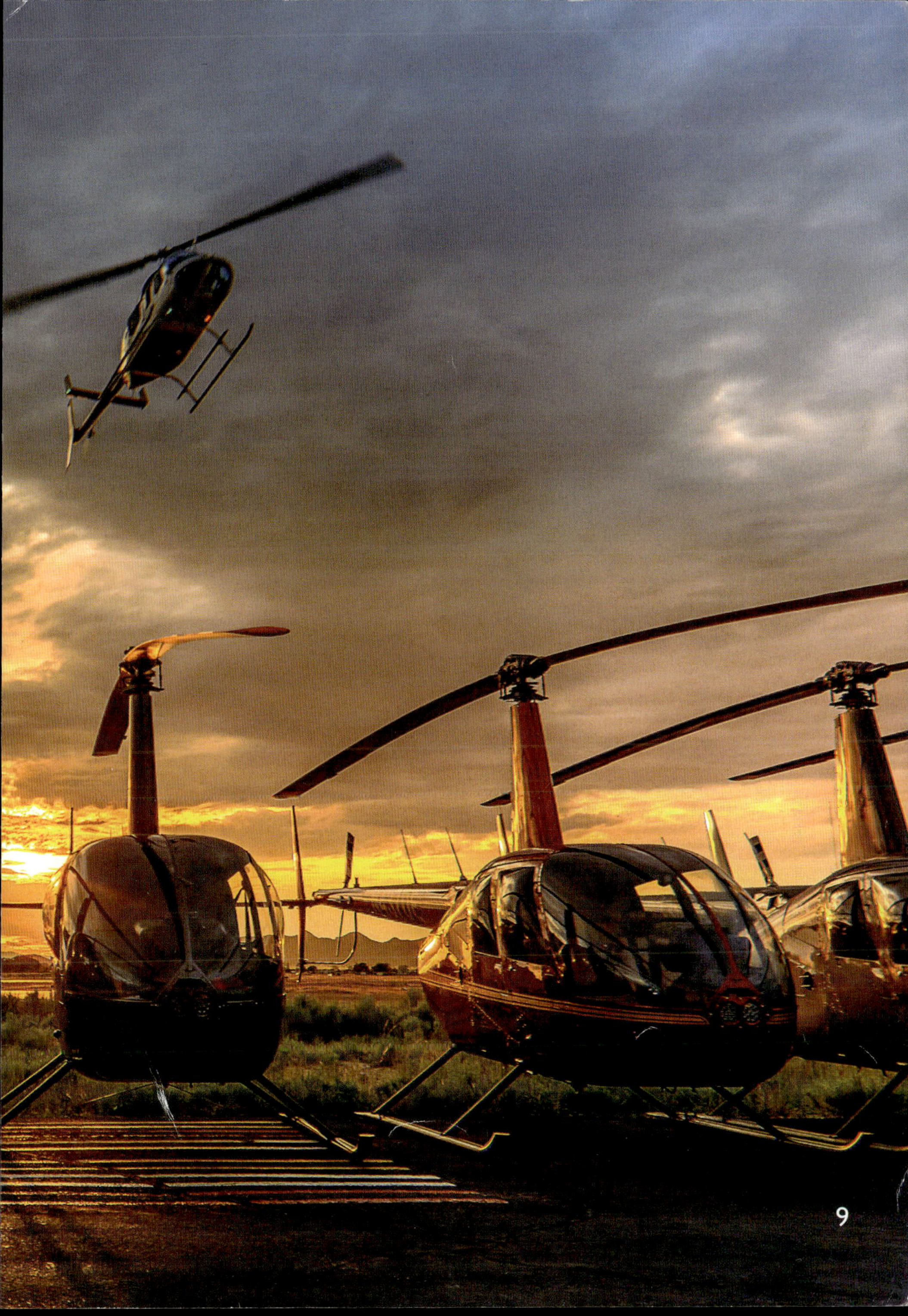

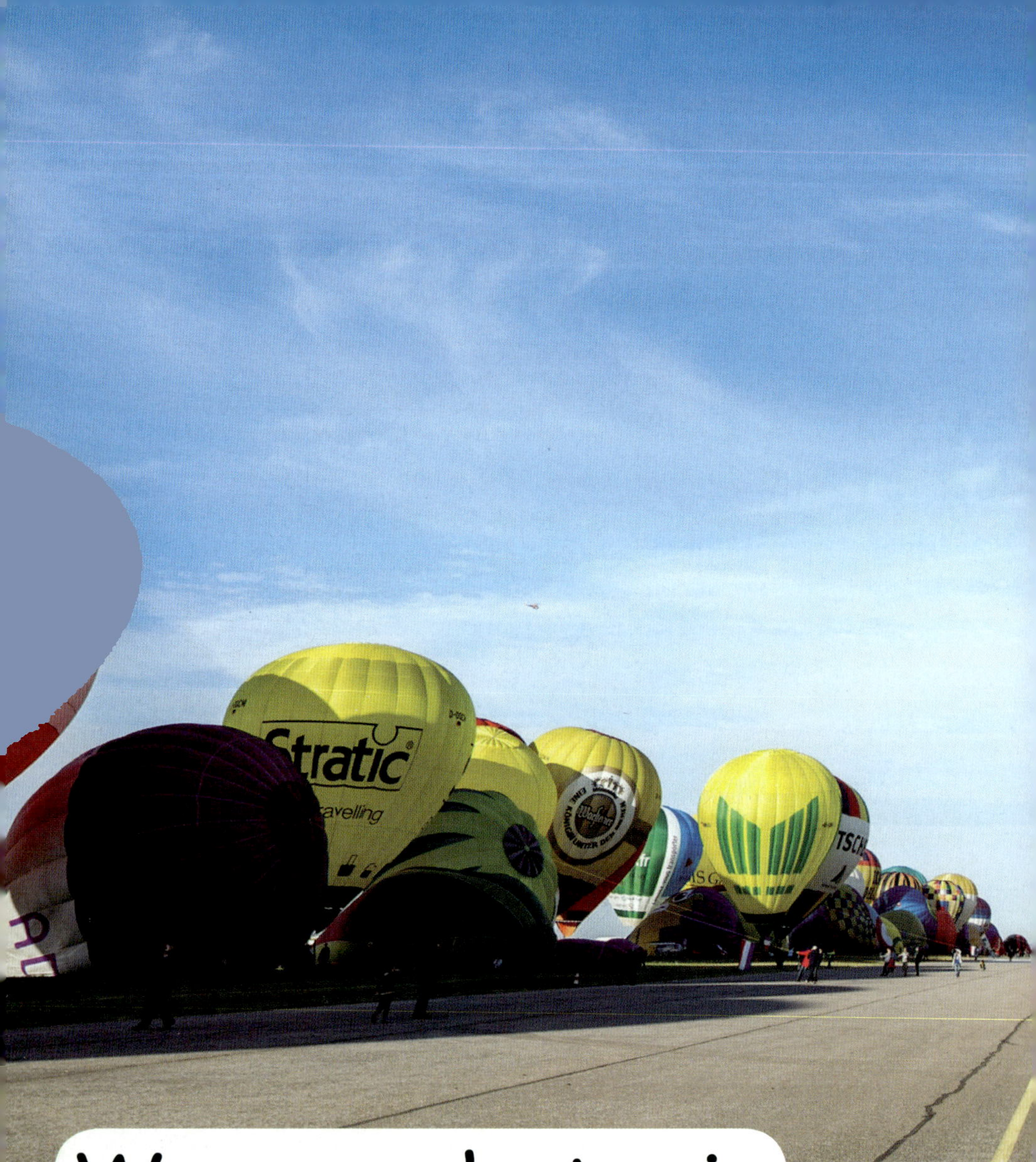

We see hot air balloons.

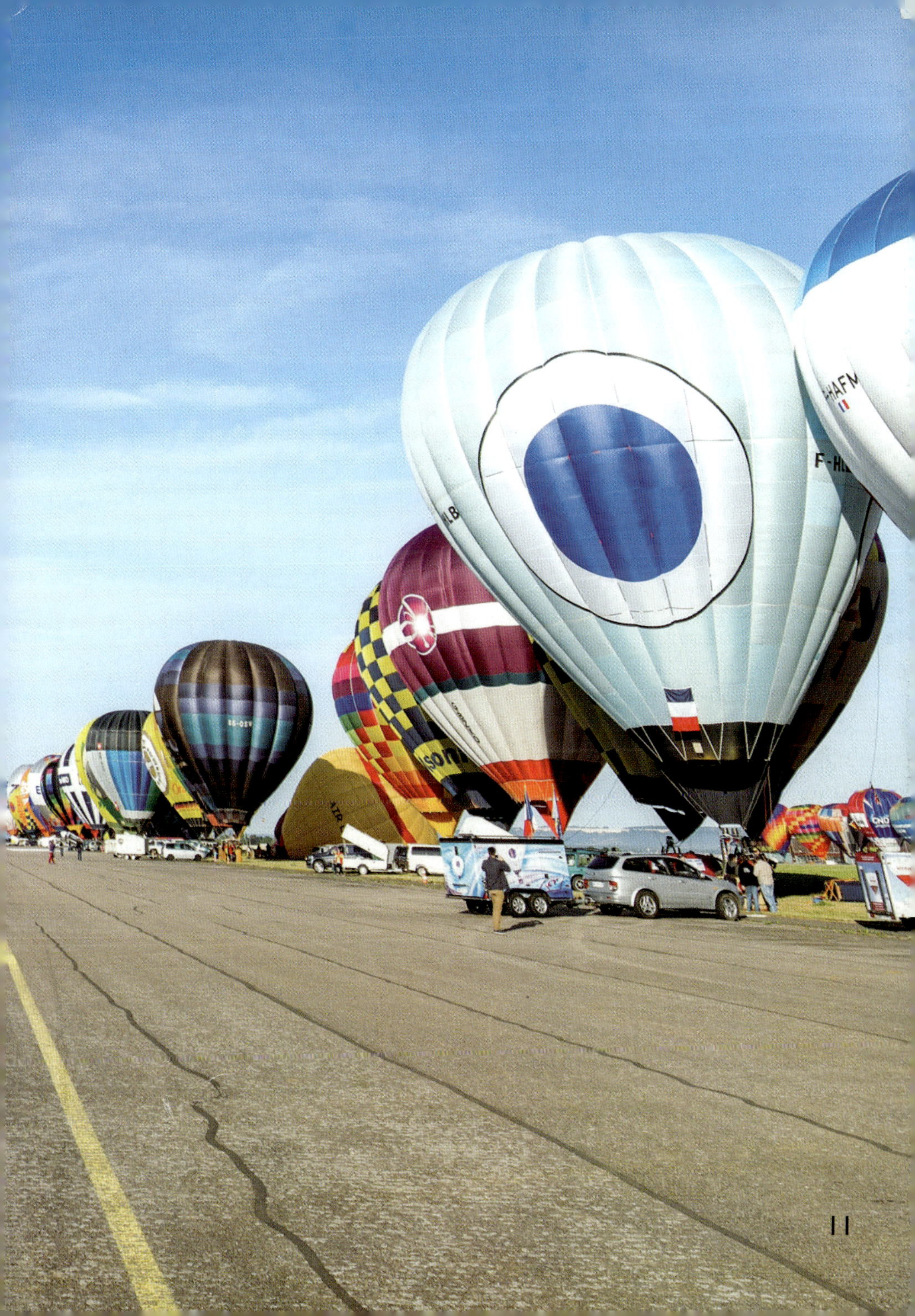

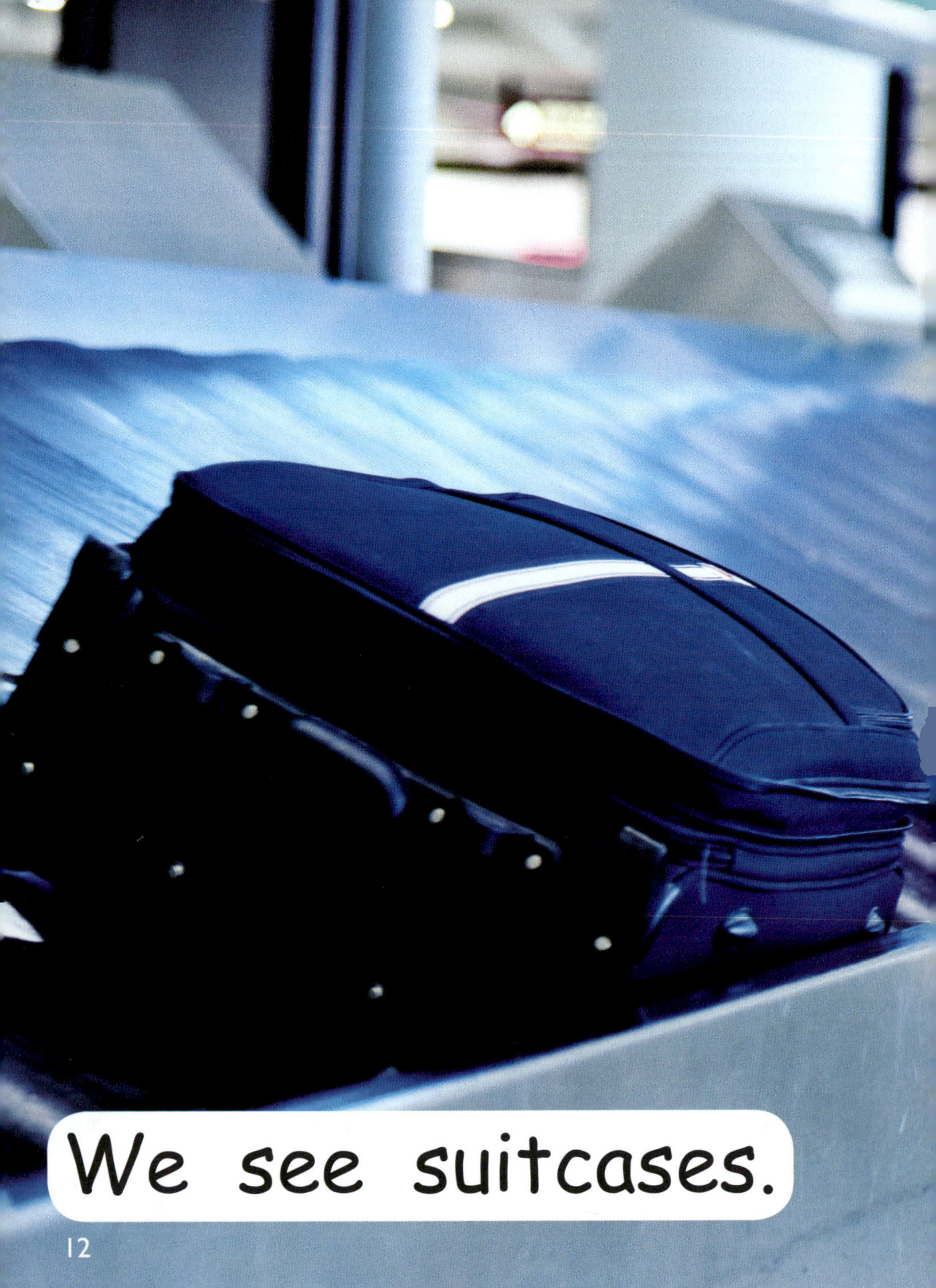

We see suitcases.

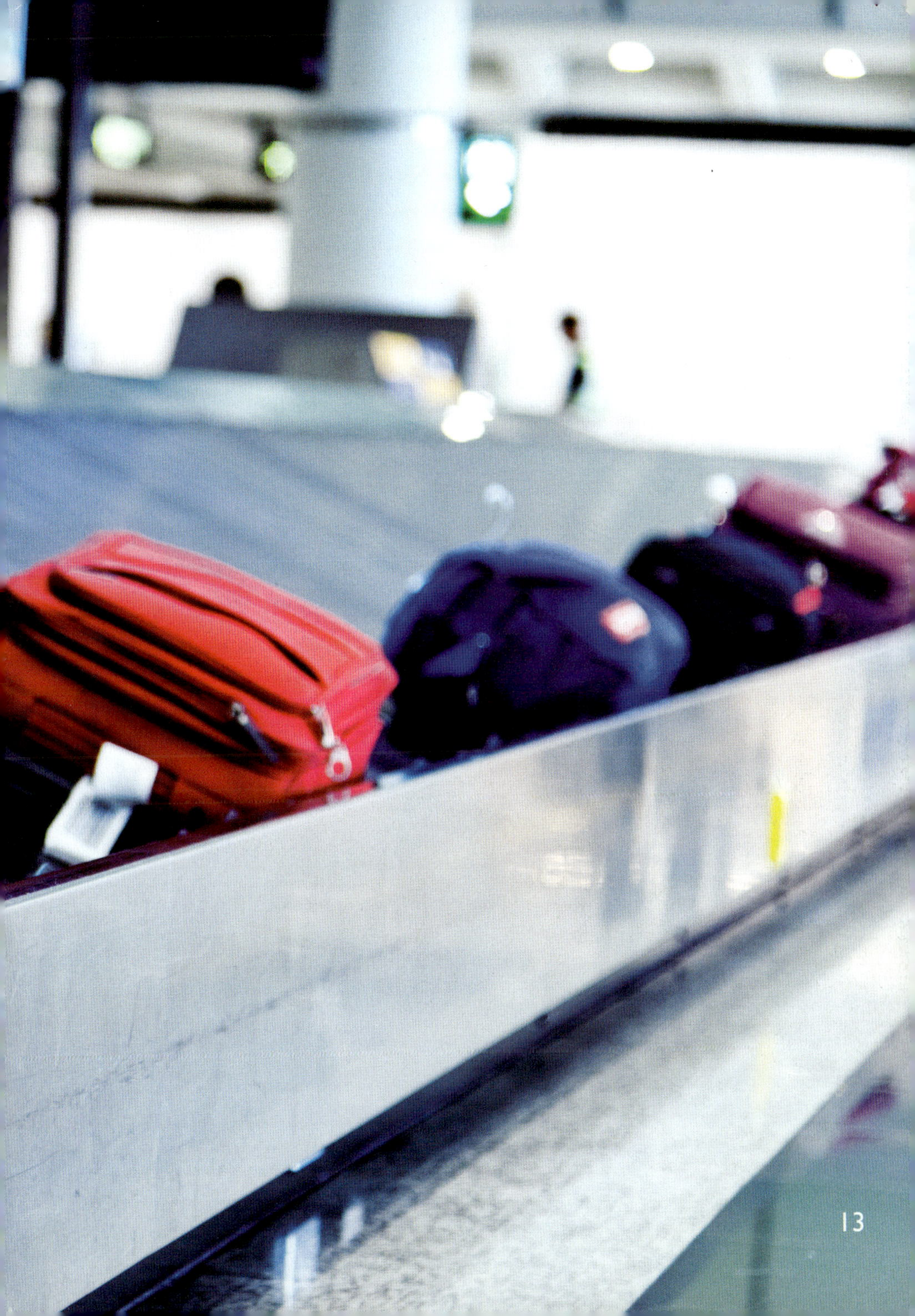

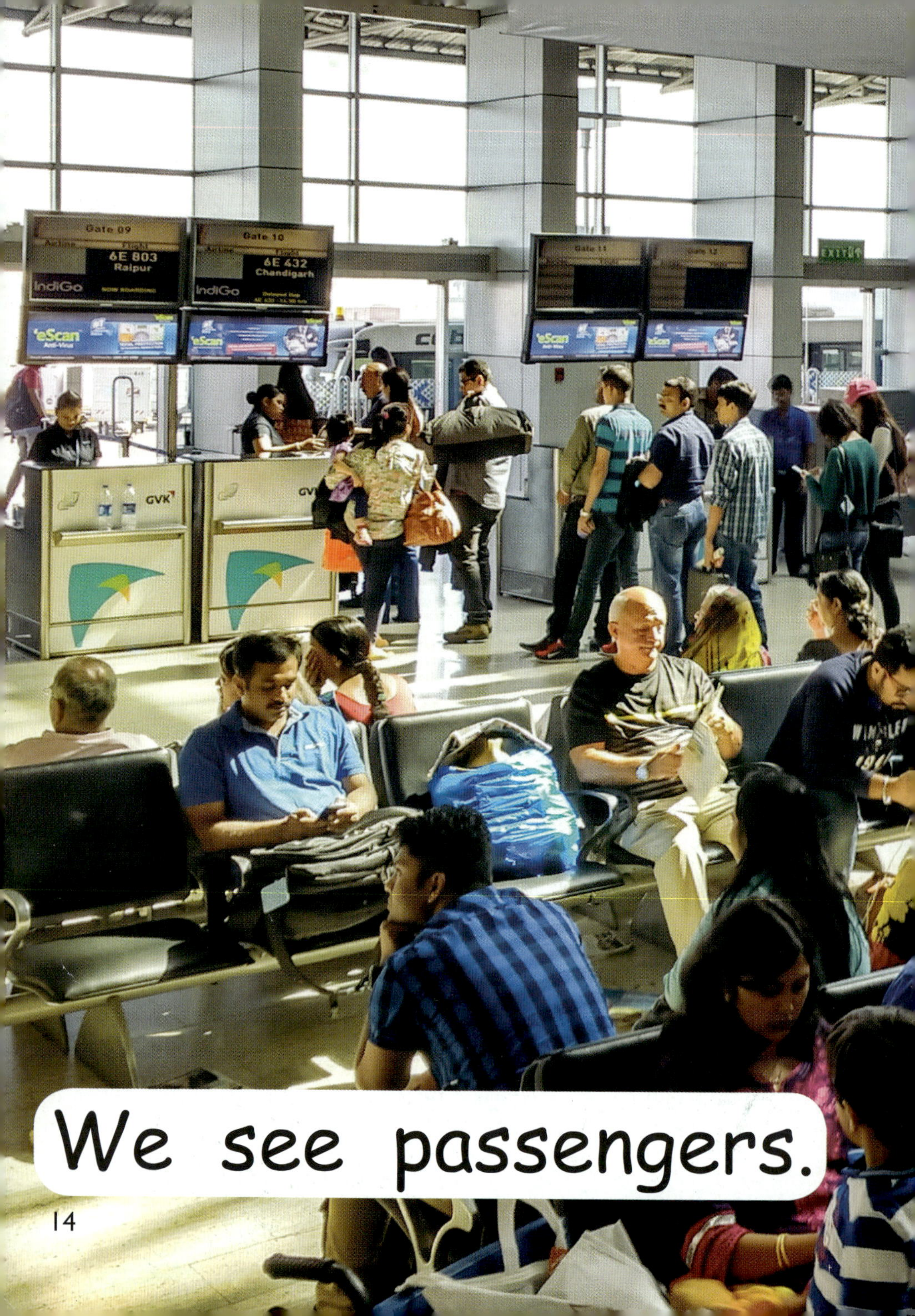

We see passengers.

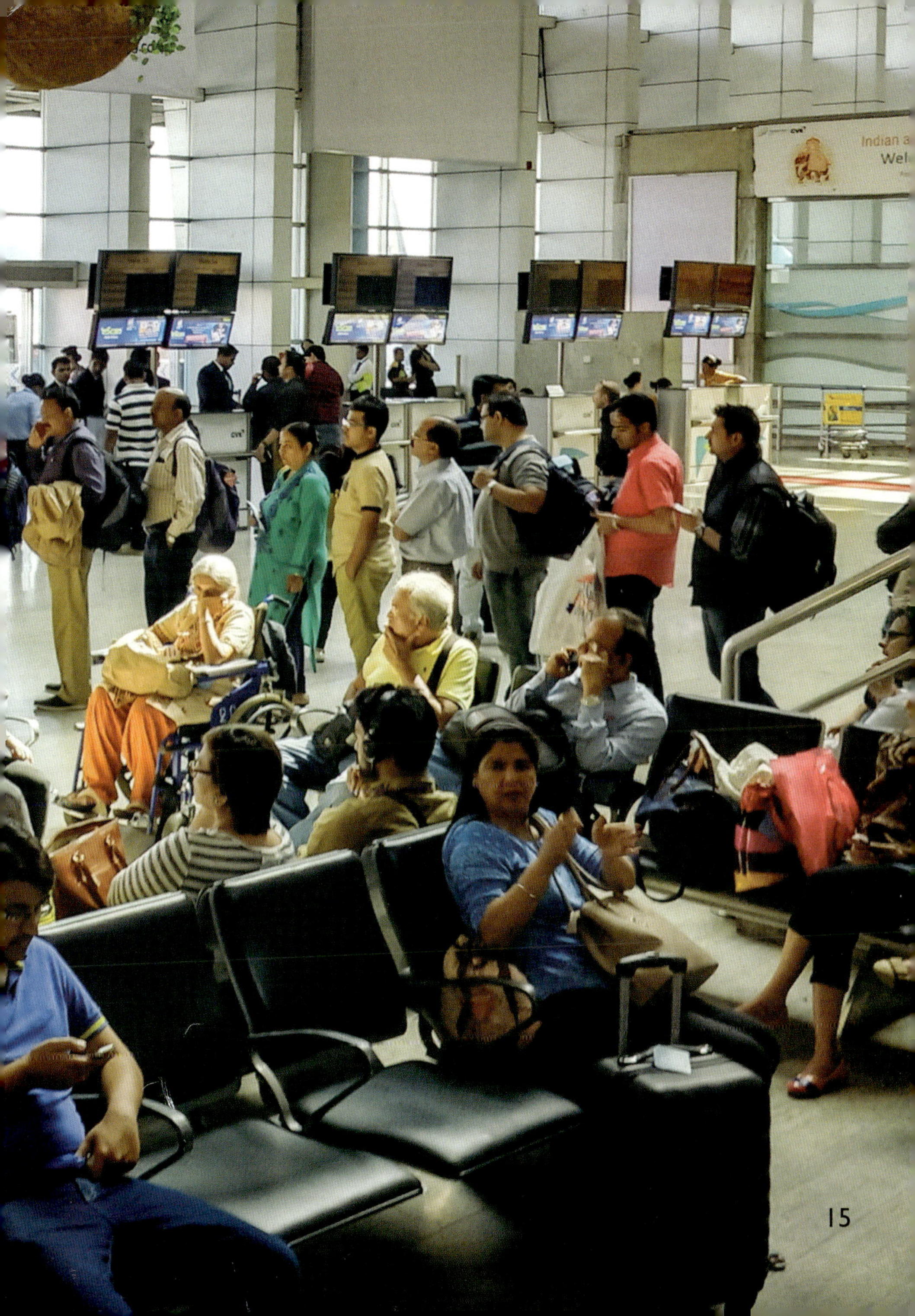

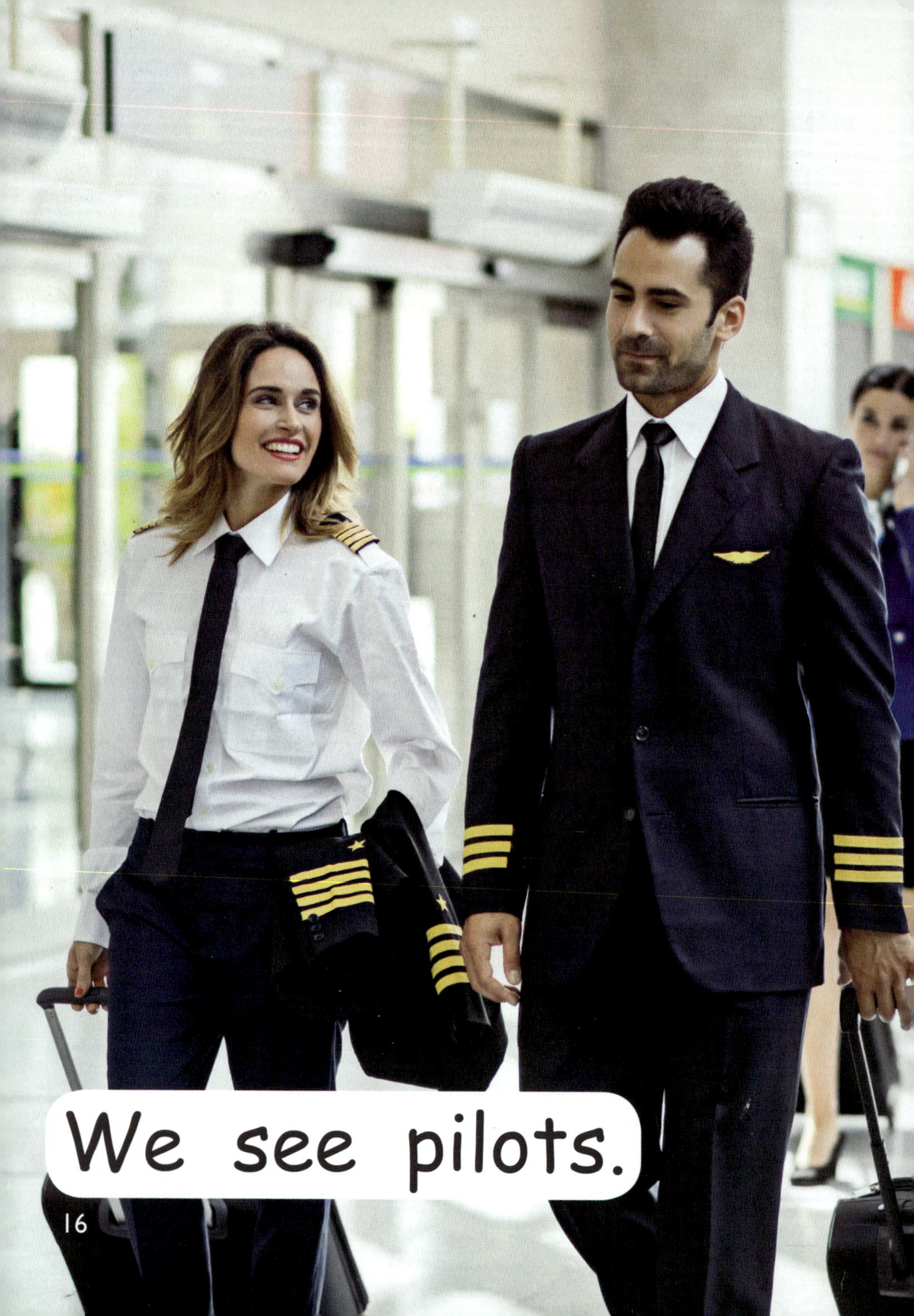

We see pilots.